BOOKKEEPING 101 FOR BUSINESS PROFESSIONALS

Increase Your Accounting Skills

And Create More Financial Stability And Wealth

Copyright © 2018 by Stephanie Horne

All rights reserved. This book or any portion thereof may not be reproduced or used in any manner whatsoever without the express written permission of the publisher except for the use of brief quotations in a book review.

Printed in the United States of America

First Printing, 2018

ISBN 9781724002723

TABLE OF CONTENTS

TABLE OF CONTENTS.. 1
ABOUT THE AUTHOR.. 4
BOOKKEEPING 101. 5
Chart of Accounts Introduction. 6
Accounts Payable Introduction. 7
Accounts Receivable Introduction. 8
Bank Reconciliation Introduction. 9
Profit and Loss Statement Introduction. 10
Balance Sheet Introduction. 11
CHART OF ACCOUNTS.. 12
Assets. 13
Liabilities. 14
Capital...15
Income or Revenue. 18
Cost of Goods Sold (COGS)...18
Expenses. 20
Other Income. 20
Other Expenses. 21
ACCOUNTS PAYABLE.. 22
Entering Open Vendor Account Balance. 24
Enter From Start Date To Today's Date. 25
A/P Register...26
Different Ways To Pay Bills. 27
A/P Video Tutorial..29
ACCOUNTS RECEIVABLE.. 32
Entering An Open Balance For A Customer.............................34
Enter From Start Date To Today's Date. 35
A/R Ledger...36
BANK RECONCILIATION.. 37
Beginning Balance. 37
Entering Initial Information. 38
Reconciling Items. 39

Other Discrepancies. 41
Balancing. 42
PROFIT AND LOSS STATEMENT. 43
Two Main Financial Statements. 44
Sample P/L Report 46
Reviewing An Income Statement 47
BALANCE SHEET. 49
B/S Account Types. 50
Sample B/S Report 52
ADDITIONAL RESOURCES.. 54
NOTES.. 55

ABOUT THE AUTHOR

Stephanie has a passion for helping people to improve their lives both personally and financially by learning new financial and personal self-help tools.

Her own personal journey has led to compiling this eBook that reveals many simple financial techniques that anyone can apply immediately for a powerful, positive money and business success transformation.

By the end of this eBook, you'll know how the need for personal self-improvement and knowledge determines the actions we should take moving forward for a better financial future.

BOOKKEEPING 101

Bookkeeping 101 For Business Professionals - Increase your accounting skills and create more financial stability and wealth will give you more than just the bookkeeping basics.

It will help teach you about many bookkeeping and accounting topics from setting up a chart of accounts to preparing your profit & loss statement.

Chart of Accounts Introduction

The chart of accounts is the foundation of your bookkeeping system, so it is very important to have a good understanding of how it works. This is a great place to get started on your learning adventure.

You can think of it like it's a file cabinet full of files, and each file will store a different kind of bookkeeping information.

So, if you have bookkeeping information for telephone payments made for your business phone line, you will set up a file (an account) for Telephone Expense.

There are many different kinds of accounts that should be included in your chart of accounts.

Accounts Payable Introduction

The accounts payable account is used to record the bills of a business that are outstanding and is also referred to as A/P which is accounts payable for short.

This is a bookkeeping 101 account that should be added to your chart of accounts the first time you enter a bill. The account will be used to track the money that your business owes to others.

When you pay off your outstanding bills, or when you enter a new bill, you should enter the transaction in the register for your A/P account.

This account is listed in the chart of accounts as accounts payable. But if you really feel you need to use more than one of this type of account in your business, then you can add additional A/P accounts to the chart or accounts.

Accounts Receivable Introduction

Accounts receivable is the term that bookkeepers and accountants use to refer to the outstanding money that is owed to you for sales that you have already made that haven't been paid for yet.

This is another bookkeeping 101 account that should be added to your chart of accounts by the first time you write an invoice. The account will be used to track the money that is owed to your business.

When you receive a payment from a customer, or when you write an invoice, you should enter the transaction in the register for your A/R account.

This account is listed in your chart of accounts as accounts receivable. But if you really need to use more than one of this type of account in your business, then you can add additional A/R accounts to the COA as well.

Bank Reconciliation Introduction

Bank reconciliation is a necessary monthly bookkeeping task for any successful business or home financial system.

There are different software programs such as QuickBooks that can help to make it easier than ever with a quick and simple process that you can learn right here.

You will learn about the importance of the beginning balance, and the ending balance and everything in between. If you have a lot of transactions, it can be helpful to maintain a checkoff system for making sure each business transaction matches in both your accounting software and your bank statement.

Profit and Loss Statement Introduction

If you are like most new business owners just starting their business, you don't know how to read financial statements. And that can be detrimental to your success. But **your business is going to be a success!**

Why? Because you are already here ready, able and willing to learn how to read and use the profit and loss statement (otherwise known as an income statement)

Balance Sheet Introduction

The balance sheet is a report that gives you a summary of the financial situation of a business on any given date. It will show you the value of your company's assets, liabilities, and equity.

There are many different bookkeeping accounts that appear on the report. The different bookkeeping accounts you will find can be thought of as all of the things (including money) that you own and the debts that you owe.

This would include things like bank accounts, property (buildings), equipment, furniture and amounts that people owe you (accounts receivable).

This also includes all of your liabilities such as bank loans, credit cards, and amounts you owe to other people (accounts payable).

CHART OF ACCOUNTS

The Chart of Accounts is the foundation of your bookkeeping system. You can think of it like it's a file cabinet full of files, and each file will store a different kind of bookkeeping information.

So, if you have bookkeeping information for telephone payments made for your business phone line, you will set up a file (an account) for Telephone Expense.

There are many different kinds of accounts that should be included in your Chart of Accounts (as shown below).

Assets

Assets are the things that your company owns. Typically they are divided into two groups: 1) current assets and 2) fixed assets.

1) Current assets are the things that you can turn easily into cash. This usually includes checking and savings accounts, money market and/or CD accounts, accounts receivable (A/R), and inventory.

2) Fixed assets are the things that you would have to sell to generate cash. (A good rule of thumb that we used at the CPA office where I worked, is anything purchased for an amount over $500.00)

Fixed Assets that are typically included in the COA are automobiles, furniture, equipment and land. An example would be if your company bought a new desk for $630. Since the cost is more than $500, it will be entered into an asset account (rather than to an expense account).

Liabilities

A liability is the money your company owes.

An example would be if your company were to borrow money from the bank. When you received the money and deposited it into the checking or savings account, the deposit would be entered as a liability account, (not an income account).

Another example would be accounts payable Any bills that come in that your company owes would be treated as a liability.

Capital

Your capital account will be set-up differently in your chart of accounts depending upon the way that your company is organized. There are three different business structures in which your business can be organized:

1) Sole proprietorship

2) Partnership

3) Corporation

1) A sole proprietorship is a single owned business that will be reported on your personal income tax return (Federal Form 1040) on the Schedule C.

A Sole proprietorship will need to set-up two main types of bookkeeping accounts.

The two types of bookkeeping accounts are:

A. Capital account

B. Owner's Drawing account.

A) The Capital account will be used to keep track of all of the money that you invest in your business from the start date of the business. And it will also include your net profits or losses each year, accumulated from when you started the business.

B) The Owner's Drawing account will be used for any money that you withdrawal from the business that is used for personal reasons.

Examples of these would be amounts you paid for groceries, personal credit cards, mortgage payments, ATM withdrawals that you are using as your wages, and any money that gets deposited into your personal accounts for any reason.

An important thing to keep in mind is that the owner of a sole proprietorship does not get a regular paycheck with money deducted for payroll taxes like an employee. Instead you will pay quarterly estimated taxes to go towards your end of year tax return.

These will be to pay your own Medicare and Social Security taxes that would normally be deducted from a paycheck.

* Please note that any quarterly estimated tax payments made from your business checking account should always be allocated to the owner's drawing account.

2) A partnership or LLP (Limited Liability Partnership) will need to set up capital and drawing accounts for each partner.

This is similar to how you would set-up the capital and draw accounts in your chart of accounts if you were a sole proprietorship. You would just add all of the same accounts for each of the partner(s) as well.

3) An "S or C corporation" or an "LLC corporation" will be set-up with a common stock account (and occasionally a preferred stock account).

Common stock and preferred stock will show the total sum of stock the company has issued.

Income or Revenue

Income and/or revenue is the money you bring in from your business which could be from products or services.

Cost of Goods Sold (COGS)

The cost of goods sold account, (also known as COGS or job costs) are all of the amounts that are applicable to running your line of business. An example of this would be if you sell some kind of product.

Your COGS would then include your cost of inventory (the amount paid for your products), any materials (used to make your product), freight charges (paid for when purchasing products), and all labor that is applicable to building the finished product.

Each of these would be set-up as a separate account under COGS in the chart of accounts.

You would also include any kind of job costs that are reimbursable expenses purchased on behalf of the customer, such as auto parts bought by a mechanic.

Expenses

Expenses (or overhead costs) are all of the fixed amounts you will have even if you run out of work. Examples of these are telephone, rent, utilities, and liability insurance.

Other Income

Other Income would be the amounts you bring in other than the normal way you do business.

Examples of these would be any interest income you get from your checking or savings accounts, any kind of gains from selling assets, money you get from insurance settlements (such as from a fire), or perhaps rental income that you bring in from renting commercial buildings that you own.

Other Expenses

Last but not least! Other Expenses are the amounts that you pay for things outside of your normal business.

Examples of these would be a loss from selling an asset or perhaps stockbroker fees from setting up or buying stock for the business.

ACCOUNTS PAYABLE

The accounts payable account is used to record the bills of a business that are outstanding and is also referred to as A/P for short.

There usually is only one single account on the chart of accounts to track all of the outstanding bills even though the word accounts is plural.

This is an account that should be added to your chart of accounts by the first time you enter a bill.

The account will be used to track the money that your business owes to others.

When you pay off your outstanding bills, or when you enter a new bill, you should enter the transaction in the register for your A/P account.

This account is listed in the chart of accounts as accounts payable." But if you really feel you need to use more than one of this type of account in your business, then you can add additional A/P accounts to the chart of accounts.

Entering Open Vendor Account Balance

For each vendor that you have, you will need to enter the amount owed to you on your start date. If you do not know the opening balance, you can just choose a different start date starting from when you do know the opening balance.

Or you can figure out the opening balance by reconstructing what you owe your vendor today and reconstruct what you owed them at your start date by subtracting any payments you made between then and now, and adding any additional billings you have received between then and now.

You can also ask your accountant for the year-to-date balances for your accounts.

When you enter the opening balance for your vendors, you're building the A/P opening balance.

Enter From Start Date To Today's Date

When you enter the following types of transactions using the standard sales forms (checks, bills and invoices) you are ensuring that your A/P accounts (and accounts receivable and income and expense statement) are up-to-date and accurate:

- Bill payments
- Bills from vendors
- Credits from vendors
- Deposits
- Sales tax payments
- Invoices and sales receipts with sales tax, if appropriate
- Customer returns
- Payments received from customers

A/P Register

The A/P register will list all of the payments, credits, and bills related to each of your individual vendors.

New bills can typically be entered directly into the register or through an enter bills tab in most bookkeeping software.

Different Ways To Pay Bills

There are two different ways that you can manage bill payments in most bookkeeping software.

You can pay bills as soon as you receive them.

You should use this method only when the bills have not been entered and you don't really need to track them.

When you pay with check, cash, or any other form of payment other than a credit card, you can use the Write Checks window.

When you pay a bill with a credit card, you should record the payment in the Enter Credit Card Charges window.

In either window, you can assign the charge to an expense account.

You can enter bills when you get them and pay them when they're due.

Using his method will let you keep your money in your business for as long as possible. It will also enable you to track how much money you owe to others.

You can then run reports at any time to see how much money you owe to others, and to whom you owe it. This is a good method to use to keep a record of all your bills, both before and after they're paid.

You can simply use the Enter Bills window to enter bills into your A/P account and use the Pay Bills window to pay them when they're due.

You can also set up most bookkeeping software to remind you to pay bills when they're due.

Important: When you enter a bill in the Enter Bills window, you should always use the Pay Bills window to pay that bill as well. If you don't do this it will not be marked as paid.

A/P Video Tutorial

View the **A/P tutorial playlist at www.bookkeeping-basics.net/accounts-payable.html.** This is a three part video series on how to do Accounts Payable in QuickBooks.

1. A/P Introduction
2. How To Do A/P In QuickBooks Part 1
3. How To Do A/P In QuickBooks Part 2

TRANSCRIBED: Hello, I'm Stephanie Horne from Bookkeeping Basics. I'm a bookkeeper and focus on professional bookkeeping services for small to medium-sized businesses. Today I will be discussing accounts payable.

So first of all, what is A/P? The accounts payable is the account that is used to record the bills of a business that are outstanding and is also referred to as A/P for short.

This is an account that should be added to your COA by the first time you enter a bill in order to properly track the money that your business owes to others.

When you enter a new bill, or you pay off your outstanding bills, you should enter the transaction in the register for your A/P account. This process may or may not start with the generation of a purchase order when you purchase something from a vendor.

After making the purchase you would then receive a bill from your vendor that you would enter into A/P so that you will be able to generate a report showing how much you owe, to who and when it's due.

Then, you would eventually pay the bill so that it would not show up in A/P. It is important to use the a/p account properly in order to generate correct reports and stay on top of cash flow.

QuickBooks accounting software makes paying and tracking bills using the a/p account nice and easy. Please come back next week and I will go over exactly how to do A/P in QuickBooks. Thank you!

ACCOUNTS RECEIVABLE

Accounts receivable is the term that bookkeepers and accountants use to refer to the outstanding money that is owed to you for sales that you have already made that haven't been paid for yet.

The account is called A/R for short. There usually is only one single account on the chart of accounts to track all of the outstanding invoices even though the word "accounts" is plural.

This is an account that should be added to your chart of accounts by the first time you write an invoice. The account will be used to track the money that is owed to your business.

When you obtain the bookkeeping services of a professional bookkeeper they will make sure this account is setup for you.

When you receive a payment from a customer, or when you write an invoice, you should enter the transaction in the register for your A/R account.

This account is listed in your chart of accounts as accounts receivable. But if you really need to use more than one of this type of account in your business, then you can add additional A/R accounts to the chart of accounts as well.

Entering An Open Balance For A Customer

For each customer that you have, you will need to enter the amount owed to you on your start date. If you do not know the opening balance, you can choose a different start date starting from when you do know the opening balance.

Or you can figure out the opening balance by reconstructing what your customers owe you today by subtracting any payments they made between then and now, and adding any additional billings between then and now.

You can also ask your accountant for the year-to-date balances for your accounts.

When you enter the opening balance for your customers, you're building the A/R opening balance.

Enter From Start Date To Today's Date

When you enter the following types of transactions using the standard sales forms (checks, bills, and invoices) you are ensuring that your A/R accounts (and A/P and P&L accounts) are up-to-date and accurate:

- Bill payments
- Bills from vendors
- Credits from vendors
- Deposits
- Sales tax payments
- Invoices and sales receipts with sales tax, if appropriate
- Customer returns
- Payments received from customers

A/R Ledger

The A/R register will list all of the payments from customers, credit memos, invoices, and customer discounts that you have entered related to each of your individual customers.

New statement charges can typically be entered directly into the register. A statement charge will appear as one item, instead of the multiple items that are shown on the invoice. You cannot enter any other transactions directly into the register.

BANK RECONCILIATION

Bank reconciliation is a necessary monthly bookkeeping task. QuickBooks makes it easier than ever with a quick and simple process that you can learn right here.

Beginning Balance

You will first select the QuickBooks accounting software file in which you will be working. Then, select Banking>Reconciliation> then the account to be reconciled. The beginning balance will be zero for a new account, or it will be carried over from a previous reconciliation.

Alternatively, if this is the first month you are using QuickBooks, it was entered when you set up the chart of accounts. Either way, it is automatically entered, and if it matches your bank statement, you are good.

Entering Initial Information

Now you should have the option to enter the statement date, ending balance, date for service charge and interest (same as statement date), and the account numbers to charge these items to. Once you have this information entered, click "continue."

Reconciling Items

After you click continue, you will see a split screen with checks and deductions on one side, and deposits and credits on the other.

Which side which is on depends on the version of QuickBooks accounting software you are using, but the columns will be labeled so you will know which is which.

If you have a lot of transactions, it can be helpful to check the box at the top that gives the option to hide all activity occurring after the end date on the bank statement you are reconciling.

Next, simply click to check off each transaction that matches your bank statement, checking each one off on the statement manually as you go.

Each item that is not checked off on the bank statement apparently did not appear in the books. It should have, so record those transactions now and check them off. Take two things first however.

Sometimes bookkeepers record a lump sum for payroll, but the banks clears individual check amounts. A payroll transit account can handle this problem easily.

Also, use credit card statements to check off credit card deposits, and then move along.

Other Discrepancies

When you are done, the ending balance on your QuickBooks file should match the ending balance on the bank statement, and the discrepancies balance in the bottom right corner of the reconciliation window should be $0.00.

If it is not, find a starting point quickly by looking at the lower left of the reconciliation window and comparing the total checks and total deposits cleared with the totals for each on the bank statement.

This can help you narrow down where to begin looking.

Balancing

Once everything is cleared, the ending balances match, and discrepancies are zero, you can prompt QuickBooks to "Reconcile Now." You will note a moment of processing and then receive a "Congratulations" message.

You can now choose to print a summary report, a detailed report, or both. It is a good idea to print both and put them with your bank statement.

If you do not, and you need a copy later, just go to Reports>Banking>Reconciliation report then follow the screen prompts.

PROFIT AND LOSS STATEMENT

The Profit and Loss Statement can tell you a lot about how a business is doing. It can also help you to determine ways that you can go about saving money (so that there is more to bring home!)

Do you know how to read *your* financial statements?

A good many new business owners who are just getting started in their own business don't know how to read the two main financial statements.

They are treating their money like it's a game.

Your business might not be operating for long if you don't learn to read and use the profit & loss statement and balance sheet.

It's a good thing you are already here to learn everything you need to know!

Two Main Financial Statements

The two main financial statements are very useful in many ways.

One beneficial thing a profit and loss statement can do is to compare the current year's income and expenses to those of the previous year. This would indicate if the decisions you are making are helping you to make more money or less money.

The balance sheet in contrast gives you a view of your overall financial health, and is an indication of whether your business is improving or if your profits are going down-hill.

The financial statements can also be used by other people in ways that can benefit you or be to your detriment. An example of this would be when you are presenting your bookkeeping reports to a bank.

The banker will look at these financial statements and try to predict how long he or she expects you to stay in business.

The profit & loss statement will basically tell the bank if your business is profitable or not. While the balance sheet will tell the bank how stable you are financially.

What you would typically want to see on a profit & loss statement would be a steady amount of growth in revenue and net income.

Sample P/L Report

A sample profit and loss report might look something like this...

Profit Loss Statement

For Dates Submitted Between: 05/01/03 and 05/31/03

INCOME

Category	
	$579.00
Car Rental	$243.00
Electric	$200.27
Food	$27.00
Lodging	$550.50
Mailing	$45.00
TOTAL INCOME	$1,644.77

Expenses

Category	
Electric	$210.00
Entertainment	$55.23
Food	$34.27
Lodging	$115.00
Travel	$455.00
TOTAL EXPENSES	$869.50
OVERALL TOTAL	$775.27

Reviewing An Income Statement

After a company does a review of its profit and loss statement, it might end up choosing not to grow in order to be able to increase their net income.

They might also decide to cut back on jobs that aren't making them as much money, or decide not to sell the types of products that are making them less money.

The Profit & Loss Statement is great to review in order to make sure that you are making money and not overspending on job costs or overhead expenses.

In contrast, on the balance sheet you would be looking for a higher amount of assets, a lower amount of liabilities, or a proportional amount of growth in assets over the liabilities.

An overall common rule of thumb is to try and keep the value of your assets at equal or at least two times the value of your liabilities. So if you have $200,000 in assets, you should have $100,000 or less in liabilities.

This would let you know that you are doing well and are right on track for the success that you seek!

BALANCE SHEET

What exactly is the balance sheet? In short, a balance sheet is a report that gives you a summary of the financial situation of a business on any given date. But what does that mean exactly?

It will show you the total value of your company's assets, liabilities and equity.

Interestingly enough, it got its name because the total of the assets is always exactly equal (*in balance*) to the combined total of the liabilities and equity.

The formula looks like this: **Assets = Liabilities + Owner's Equity.** This is also otherwise known as the Accounting Equation.

B/S Account Types

There are many different bookkeeping accounts that appear on the monthly and annual report.

The different bookkeeping accounts you will find can be thought of as all of the things (including money) that you own as well as all of the debts that you owe.

This would include things like bank accounts, property (buildings), equipment, furniture, and amounts that people owe you (accounts receivable).

This also includes all of your liabilities such as bank loans, credit cards, and amounts you owe to other people (accounts payable).

Additional types of bookkeeping accounts that you will find are the equity accounts. These indicate what your business is worth and include all of the money (investments) that the owners have put into the company as well as all of the money, draws or distributions that the owners take back out.

The equity of your company is the total of all of your assets (what you own) minus the total of all of your liabilities (what you owe). This is also known as the net worth of your company.

When determining what you equity is, the accounting formula changes. Now the formula would look like this: Equity = Assets - Liabilities.

Sample B/S Report

Your b/s report may be long or short depending up the type of company you have, how many assets, furniture, equipment, and loans you have.

However a report will always have the same overall look and feel. A sample report might look something like this...

BALANCE SHEET
ASSETS

Current Assets	
Cash	$ 710,000
Receivables	2,379,000
Inventories	3,361,000
Prepaid Expenses	43,000
Total Current Assets	6,493,000
Other Investments	5,111,000
Property, Buildings and Equipment	5,227,000
TOTAL ASSETS	**16,831,000**

LIABILITIES AND PATRON EQUITIES

Current Liabilities	
Short-Term Notes Payable	1,800,000
Current Portion of Long-Term Debt	367,000
Payables and Accruals	1,775,000
Total Current Liabilities	3,942,000
Long-Term Debt	1,082,000
TOTAL LIABILITIES	**5,024,000**
TOTAL PATRON EQUITIES	**11,807,000**
TOTAL LIABILITIES AND PATRON EQUITIES	**16,831,000**

ADDITIONAL RESOURCES

www.Bookkeeping-Basics.net/accounting-definitions-glossary.html

www.Bookkeeping-Basics.net/accounting-definitions-wordsearch.html

www.Bookkeeping-Basics.net/accounting-definitions-ecourse.html

www.facebook.com/HorneFinancialServices

www.twitter.com/hornefncl

www.pinterest.com/hornefncl

NOTES

www.ingramcontent.com/pod-product-compliance
Lightning Source LLC
Chambersburg PA
CBHW031928240526
45464CB00023B/2705